I Had

a

Pet Frog

Coloring Book

Pets and animals with English and Chinese words

I Had

a

Pet Frog
Coloring Book

Pets and animals with English and Chinese words

青蛙

Illustrations by Christine Liao

Text by Dr. Wan-Yu Chao and Ronald Kerble

I Had a Pet Frog Co.

Library of Congress Control Number: 2010905663

ISBN: 9780982713310

Cover design by Dr. Wan-Yu Chao & Ronald Kerble
Cover illustration by Christine Liao

Attention: Schools, Businesses and Clubs:
This book is available at a quantity discount with bulk purchase for educational, business, fundraising or sales promotional use.
For information, please email to the publisher at
<u>customerservice@ihadapetfrog.com</u>

From our family to your family
with our love of animals and
a sense of humor

從我們的家庭到您的家庭
謹獻上我們對動物之愛和幽默感

We would love for you to send us a copy of your children's work, so we can add their creative drawings to our website
at
www.ihadapetfrog.com.

Send them to
customerservice@ihadapetfrog.com

**See Dr. Wan-Yu Chao & Ronald Kerble's
other publications**

I Had a Pet Frog
*100 pets and animals that will make you smile,
chuckle and laugh out loud*

I Had a Pet Frog Calendar

How to Make a Christmas North Pole Decoration
**The ultimate holiday decoration project for families,
clubs, youth groups, schools & churches**

I Had a Pet Frog T-shirts

@ www.ihadapetfrog.com

Frog 青蛙 (CHIN WAH)

Duck 鴨 (YAH)

Hyena　　　鬣狗 **(LEAH GO)**

Cow　　母牛 (MOO NEO)

Bear   熊 (SHOWN)

Snake 蛇 (SHUH)

Toad 蟾蜍 (CHAN CHEW)

Giraffe 長頸鹿 (CHONG GING LOO)

Horse　　　馬 (MAH)

Bird 鳥 **(NEOW)**

Cat 貓 (MAO)

Turtle 龜 (GUAY)

Octopus　　章魚 **(JUNG YOU)**

Eel　　　電鰻 **(DEE-AN MINE)**

　　　14

Chameleon　　　變色龍 **(BEE-AN SAH LONE)**

Mosquito　　　　蚊子 **(WON ZEH)**

Cow 母牛 (MOO NEO)

Porcupine　箭豬 (GEE-AN JEU)

Rhinoceros 犀牛 **(SHEE NEO)**

Dalmatian 狗 (GO)

Boa constrictor　　蟒蛇 **(MONG SHUH)**

Elephant 大象 **(DAH SHUN)**

Lobster　　　龍蝦 **(LONE SHAH)**

Alligator 鱷魚 **(UGH YOU)**

Jellyfish 水母 **(SHRAY MOO)**

Lion　　　獅子　**(SHER ZEH)**

　　　26

Dog 狗 (GO)

Poot

Sheep 羊 **(YOUNG)**

Squid　　　　魷魚 (YO YOU)

Raptor   恐龍 (CONE LONE)

Snail 蝸牛 **(GUAH NEO)**

Cat 貓 **(MAO)**

Canary 金絲雀 **(GEEN SIH CHEH)**

33

Monkey 猴子 **(HO ZIH)**

Dragon 龍 (LONE)

Kitten　　　小貓 **(SHAO MAO)**

　　　36

Penguin　　　企鵝 **(CHEE UGH)**

Pig 豬 (JEU)

Hen　　母雞 (MOO GEE)

Piglets　　　小豬 (SHAO JEU)

Cyclops　　獨眼巨人 **(DEUL YEN JEU-AN)**

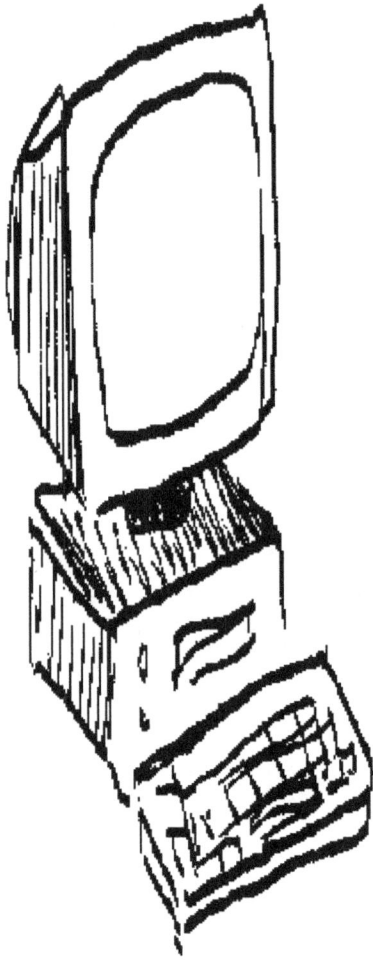

Parrot 鸚鵡 (ING WOO)

Firefly 螢火蟲 (ING WHAH CHONG)

Eagle 鷹 **(ING)**

Tiger 虎 (WHO)

45

Shark 鯊魚 **(SHAH YOU)**

Rabbit 兔 (TWO)